ESSENTIAL ELEMENTS for Band

COMPREHENSIVE BAND METHOD

TIM LAUTZENHEISER • JOHN HIGGINS • CHARLES MENGHINI
PAUL LAVENDER • TOM C. RHODES • DON BIERSCHENK

To create an account, visit:
www.essentialelementsinteractive.com

Student Activation Code
E2EB-3788-7364-7446

ISBN 979-835013704-0

REVIEW
KEY SIGNATURE
Key of B♭
TIME SIGNATURES
A
B♭
C
D
E♭
F
G
NOTES
RESTS
Whole
Half
Quarter
Eighths
REPEAT SIGN
TIE
TEMPO MARKINGS
Allegro
Moderato
1. TECHNIQUE TRAX
2. WELCOME SONG
African Folk Song
Allegro
mf
3. THAILAND LULLABY
Thai Folk Song
Moderato
4. SHEPHERD'S HEY
English Folk Song
Moderato
5. THE CRAWDAD SONG
American Folk Song
Allegro

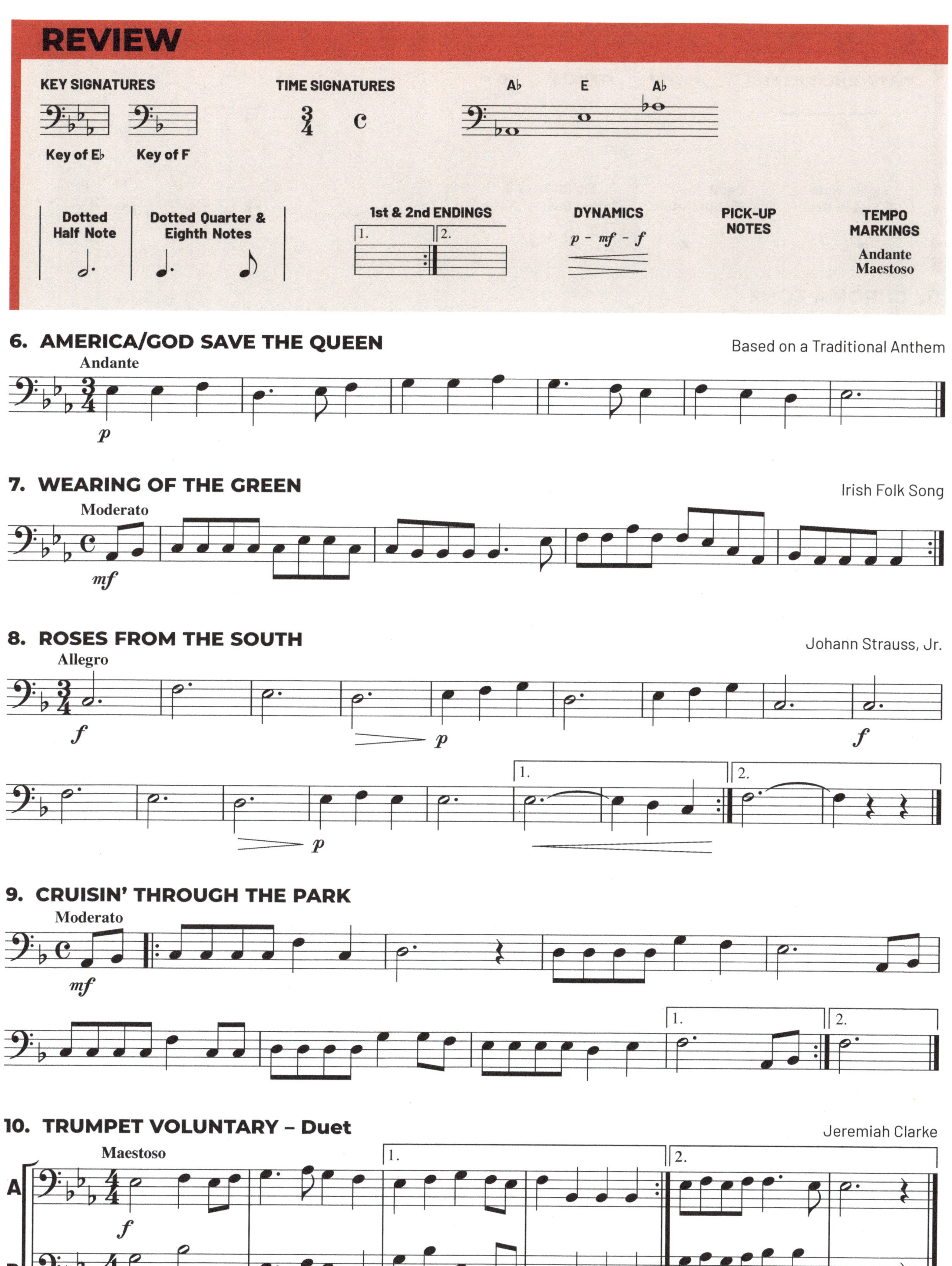
REVIEW
KEY SIGNATURES
Key of E♭
Key of F
TIME SIGNATURES
A♭
E
A♭
Dotted Half Note
Dotted Quarter & Eighth Notes
1st & 2nd ENDINGS
DYNAMICS
p - mf - f
PICK-UP NOTES
TEMPO MARKINGS
Andante
Maestoso
6. AMERICA/GOD SAVE THE QUEEN
Based on a Traditional Anthem
Andante
7. WEARING OF THE GREEN
Irish Folk Song
Moderato
8. ROSES FROM THE SOUTH
Johann Strauss, Jr.
Allegro
9. CRUISIN' THROUGH THE PARK
Moderato
10. TRUMPET VOLUNTARY – Duet
Jeremiah Clarke
Maestoso
A
B

REVIEW

MULTIPLE MEASURE REST 2

ACCENT >

FERMATA

D.C. al FINE

A B♭ C

Eighth Note & Eighth Rest

Eighth Rest & Eighth Note

Eighth Note & Dotted Quarter Note

ENHARMONICS C♯ D♭ F♯ G♭

11. CHROMA-ZONE

12. BILLY BOY

American Folk Song

13. TECHNIQUE TRAX

14. SALSA SIESTA – Duet

Staccato

Staccato notes are played lightly and with separation. They are marked with a dot above or below the note.

15. TREADING LIGHTLY

Moderato

Tenuto

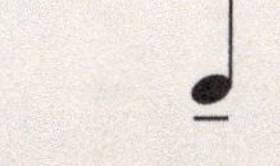

Tenuto notes are played smoothly and connected, holding each note until the next is played. They are marked with a straight line above or below the note.

Slur

A curved line which connects notes of different pitch.

Hammer on Is achieved by plucking the first note of a slurred passage with the right hand, then pressing down the second note with the left hand.

Pull off Is achieved by plucking the first note of a slurred passage with the right hand, then releasing the first note with the left hand enabling the second note to ring.

16. SMOOTH MOVE

Moderato

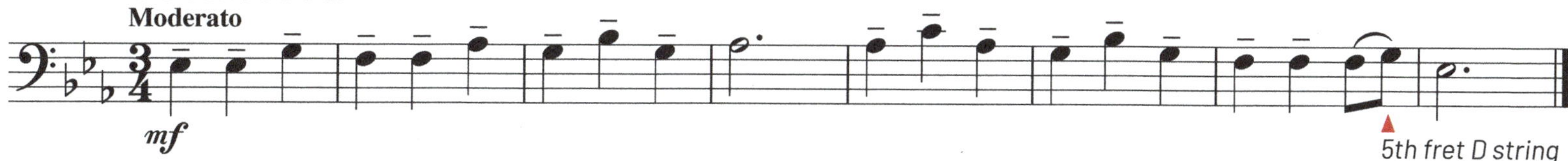

17. SHIFTING GEARS

Moderato

HISTORY

English composer **Thomas Tallis** (1508–1585) served as a royal court composer for Kings Henry VIII and Edward VI, and Queens Mary and Elizabeth. During Tallis' lifetime, the artist Michelangelo painted the Sistine Chapel.

Canons (one or more parts imitating the first part) were used in many forms by 16th century composers. A **Round** is a strict (or exact) canon which can be repeated any number of times without stopping. Play *Tallis Canon* as a 4-part round.

18. TALLIS CANON (Round)

Thomas Tallis

Moderato

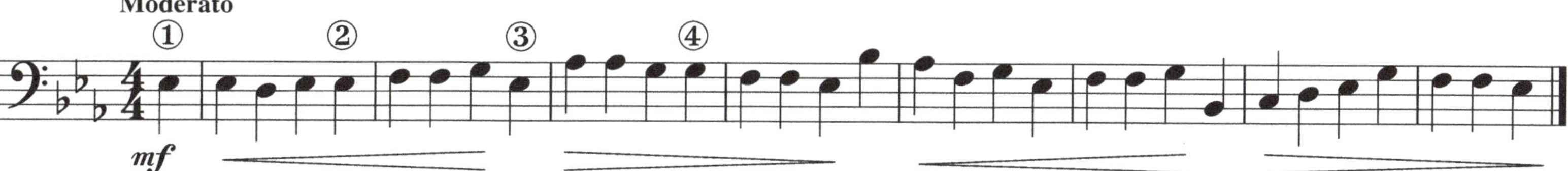

Sightreading

Sightreading means playing a musical piece for the first time. The key to sightreading success is to know what to look for *before* you play. Use the word **S-T-A-R-S** to remind yourself what to look for, and eventually your band will become sightreading STARS!

- **S** – **Sharps or flats** in the key signature
- **T** – **Time signature** and **tempo markings**
- **A** – **Accidentals** not found in the key signature
- **R** – **Rhythms**, silently counting the more difficult notes and rests
- **S** – **Signs**, including dynamics, articulations, repeats and endings

19. SIGHTREADING CHALLENGE

Moderato

DAILY WARM-UPS

WORK-OUTS FOR TONE & TECHNIQUE

20. TONE BUILDER

21. FLEXIBILITY STUDY

22. TECHNIQUE TRAX

▲ 5th fret A string

▲ 5th fret D string ▲

23. CHORALE

Johann Sebastian Bach

Andante

p

▼ 5th fret A string

▼ 5th fret A string

mf

p

24. GRANDFATHER'S CLOCK

Henry C. Work

Ritardando *ritard.* (or) *rit.* – Gradually slower.

25. GLOW WORM

Paul Lincke

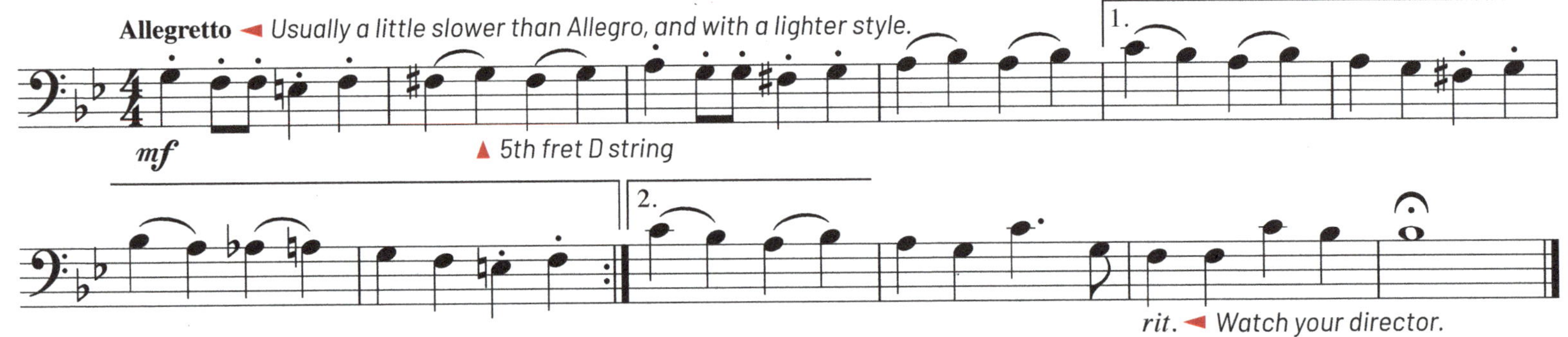

26. ALMA MATER – New Note

Practice long tones on all new notes.

A.C. Weekes, W.M. Smith, H.S. Thompson

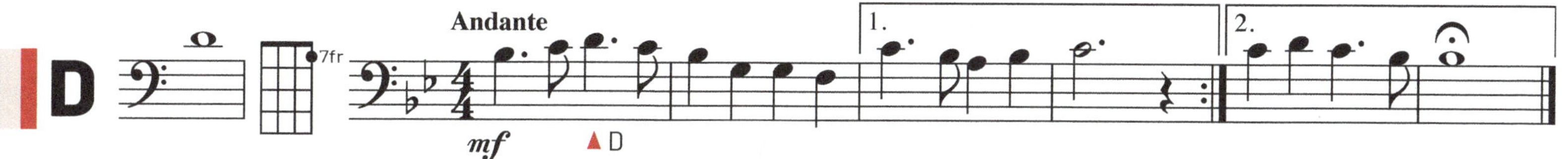

The Scottish folk song *Loch Lomond* is credited to an anonymous soldier who was imprisoned and awaiting execution. In it he writes of his desire to return home to his family and the breathtaking beauty of Loch (Lake) Lomond, a lake in Scotland. Located in the southern highlands, the lake is almost entirely surrounded by hills. One of these is Ben Lomond, a peak 3,192 feet high.

27. LOCH LOMOND

Scottish Folk Song

Key Changes

If a key signature changes during a piece of music, you will usually see a thin double bar line at the **key change**. You may also see natural signs reminding you to "cancel" previous sharps or flats. Keep playing, using the correct notes indicated in the *new* key signature.

28. MOLLY MALONE

Irish Folk Song

Dynamics

cresc. = *crescendo* (or) [crescendo hairpin]

decresc. = *decrescendo* (or) [decrescendo hairpin]

29. RISE AND FALL

30. NO COMPARISON

31. SIGHTREADING CHALLENGE

Remember the S-T-A-R-S guidelines.

THEORY

¢ Time Signature
Cut Time (Alla Breve)

¢ or $\frac{2}{2}$ = **2 beats** per measure
= **Half** note gets one beat

𝅝 = 2 beats
𝅗𝅥 = 1 beat
♩ = ½ beat

32. RHYTHM RAP *Clap the rhythm while counting and tapping.*

Clap

1 & 2 & 1 & 2 & 1 & 2 & 1 & 2 & 1 & 2 & 1 & 2 & 1 & 2 & 1 & 2 &

33. A CUT ABOVE

1 & 2 & 1 & 2 & 1 & 2 & 1 & 2 & 1 & 2 & 1 & 2 & 1 & 2 & 1 & 2 &

34. TWO-FOUR YANKEE DOODLE

American Folk Song

Moderato

mf

35. CUT TIME YANKEE DOODLE

American Folk Song

Moderato

mf

36. MARIANNE

Jamaican Folk Song

37. THE VICTORS

Louis Elbel

38. ESSENTIAL CREATIVITY *Write this example in cut time ¢ before playing.*

Dynamics

mp — *mezzo piano* (moderately soft)

These are the four dynamic levels you've learned.
p – mp – mf – f

39. A - ROVING

Syncopation

Syncopation occurs when an accent or emphasis is given to a note that is not on a strong beat. This type of "off-beat" feel is common in many popular and classical styles.

THEORY

40. RHYTHM RAP

41. IN SYNC

42. LA ROCA

Puerto Rican Folk Song

American composer **George M. Cohan** (1878–1942) was also a popular author, producer, director and performer. He helped develop a popular form of American musical theater now known as musical comedy. He is also considered to be one of the most famous composers of American patriotic songs, earning the Congressional Medal of Honor in 1917 for his song *Over There*. Many of his songs became morale boosters when the United States entered World War I in that same year.

HISTORY

43. ESSENTIAL ELEMENTS QUIZ – YOU'RE A GRAND OLD FLAG

Words and Music by George M. Cohan

THEORY

New Key Signature

This key signature indicates your **Key of C** (no flats or sharps).

44. KEY MOMENT – New Note *Try the C Scale wihtout using open strings.*

B

C Scale — B — *Arpeggio*

45. THE MINSTREL BOY

Irish Folk Song

Andante

mp

1. 2.

46. CLOSE CALL – New Note

B

B

1. 2.

47. VICTORY MARCH

M. J. Shea

March Tempo

f

1. 2.

THEORY

Cut Time Syncopation

$\frac{2}{4}$ ♪ ♩ ♪ = ¢ ♩ 𝅗𝅥 ♩

Compare the notation of the melody below with *Victory March* above. Should they sound the same?

48. WINNING STREAK

M. J. Shea

49. SIGHTREADING CHALLENGE *Remember the S-T-A-R-S guidelines.*

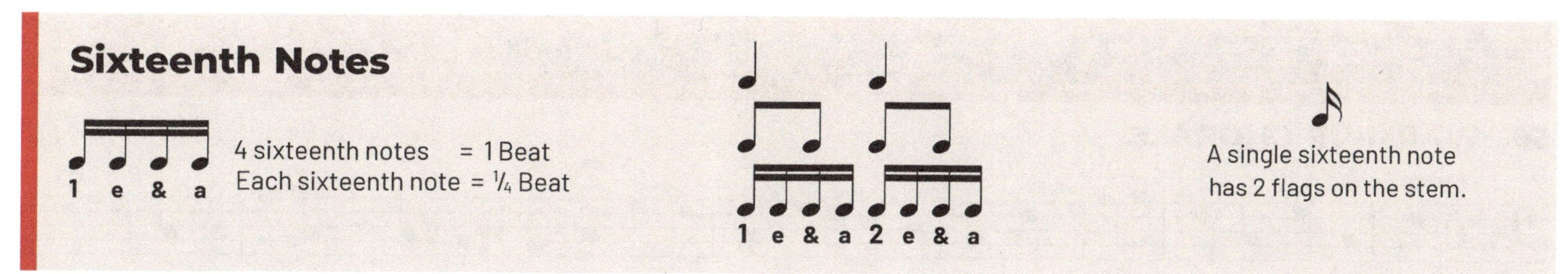

50. RHYTHM RAP

51. SIXTEENTH NOTE FANFARE

52. MOVING ALONG

53. BACK AND FORTH – Duet

54. COMIN' ROUND THE MOUNTAIN VARIATIONS

American Folk Song

55. ESSENTIAL ELEMENTS QUIZ

PERFORMANCE SPOTLIGHT
56. WARM-UP CHORALE
J. S. Bach/Arr. by John Higgins
Largo
p
mp
p
rit.
5th fret D string
57. THE THUNDERER – Band Arrangement
John Philip Sousa
Arr. by John Higgins
March style
mf cresc.
f
5
13
Fine
D.C. al Fine
mf
Reproduced by Permission of Boosey & Hawkes Music Publishers Ltd.
58. HILL AND GULLY RIDER – Band Arrangement
Jamaican Folk Song
Arr. by John Higgins
Moderato
2
3
7
11
f
mf
1.
2.
p
59. SHENANDOAH – Band Arrangement
American Folk Song
Arr. by John Higgins
Largo
5
11
p
mf
p rit.

PERFORMANCE SPOTLIGHT
60. LAS MAÑANITAS – Band Arrangement
Mexican Folk Song
Arr. by John Higgins
Allegro
3
11
19
cresc.
1.
2.
61. RONDEAU – Band Arrangement
Jean-Joseph Mouret
Arr. by John Higgins
March Style
1.
2.
Fine
D.S. al Fine
62. ROCK.COM – Encore Band Arrangement
John Higgins
Moderato
9
1.
2.

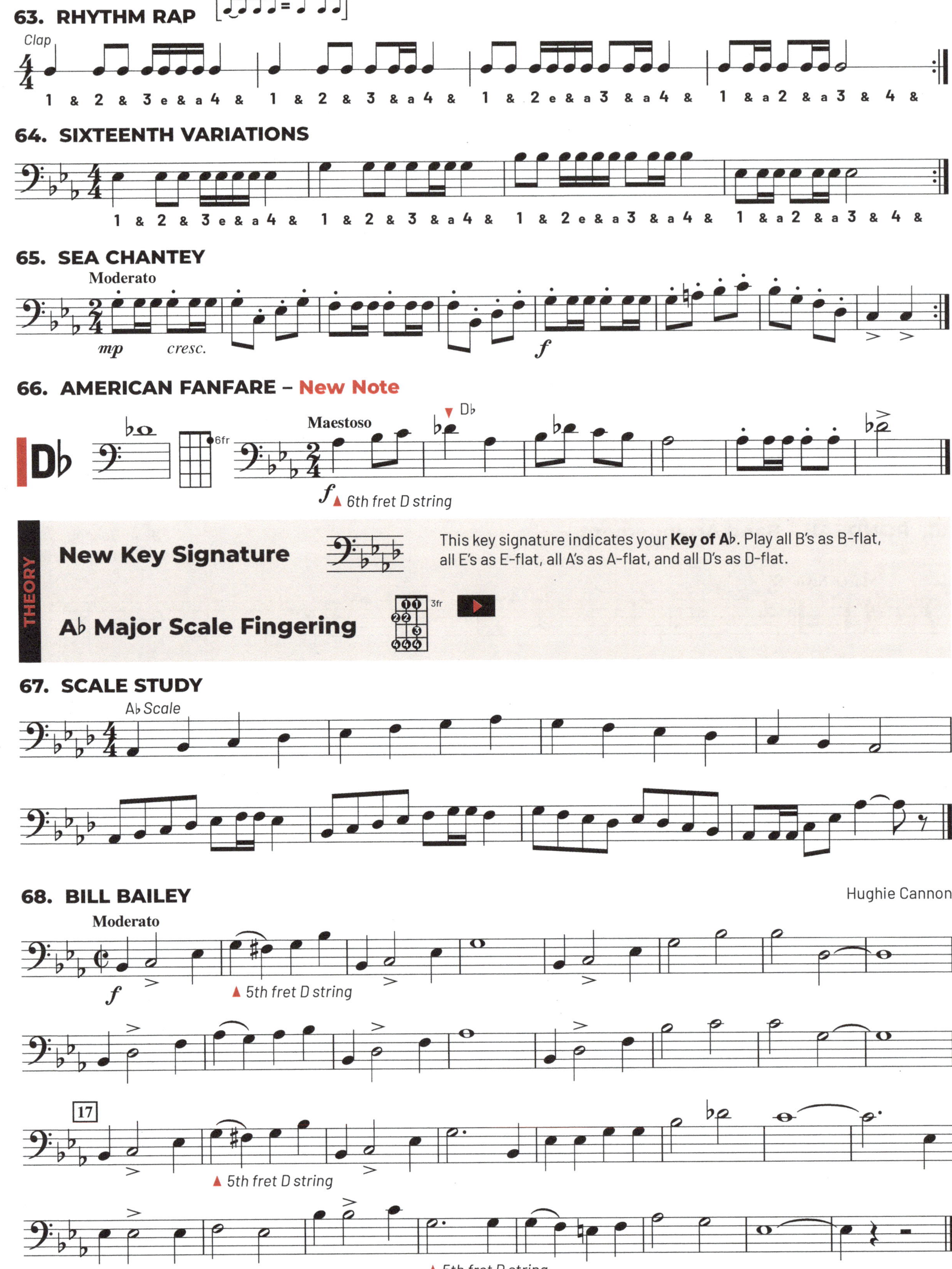
63. RHYTHM RAP
Clap
1 & 2 & 3 e & a 4 & 1 & 2 & 3 & a 4 & 1 & 2 e & a 3 & a 4 & 1 & a 2 & a 3 & 4 &
64. SIXTEENTH VARIATIONS
1 & 2 & 3 e & a 4 & 1 & 2 & 3 & a 4 & 1 & 2 e & a 3 & a 4 & 1 & a 2 & a 3 & 4 &
65. SEA CHANTEY
Moderato
mp
cresc.
f
66. AMERICAN FANFARE – New Note
D♭
6fr
Maestoso
D♭
f
6th fret D string
THEORY
New Key Signature
This key signature indicates your Key of A♭. Play all B's as B-flat, all E's as E-flat, all A's as A-flat, and all D's as D-flat.
A♭ Major Scale Fingering
3fr
67. SCALE STUDY
A♭ Scale
68. BILL BAILEY
Hughie Cannon
Moderato
f
5th fret D string
17
5th fret D string
5th fret D string

69. RHYTHM RAP

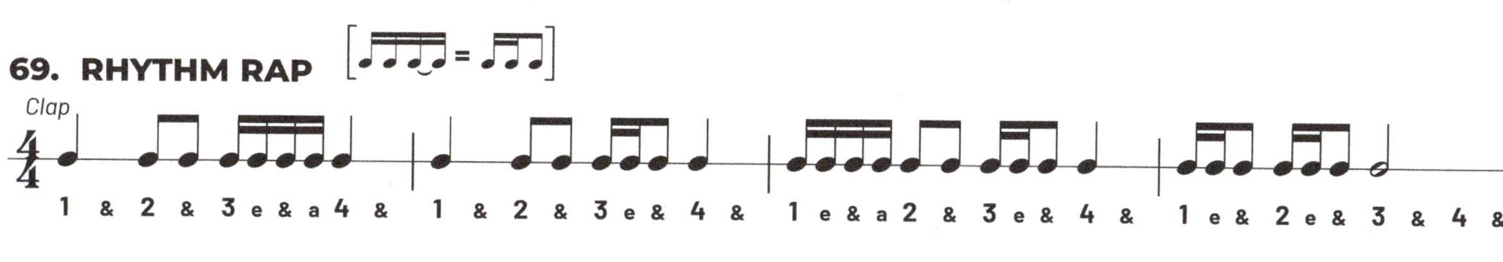

70. RHYTHM ETUDE

71. BATTLE STATIONS

72. ENGLISH DANCE *Try using only 3rd fret through 6th fret positions.*

73. BIG ROCK CANDY MOUNTAIN

American Folk Song

74. ESSENTIAL ELEMENTS QUIZ *Use A♭ major scale fingering.*

Looking for some more fun music to play?
See the inside front cover for instructions on accessing recent popular Bonus Songs.

Rallentando *rall.* – Gradually slower (same as *ritardando*).

75. SIMPLE SONG – Duet

76. LINE DANCE

77. TECHNIQUE TRAX

78. THE GALWAY PIPER

Irish Reel

79. MANHATTAN BEACH MARCH

John Philip Sousa

80. SIGHTREADING CHALLENGE

Remember the S-T-A-R-S guidelines.

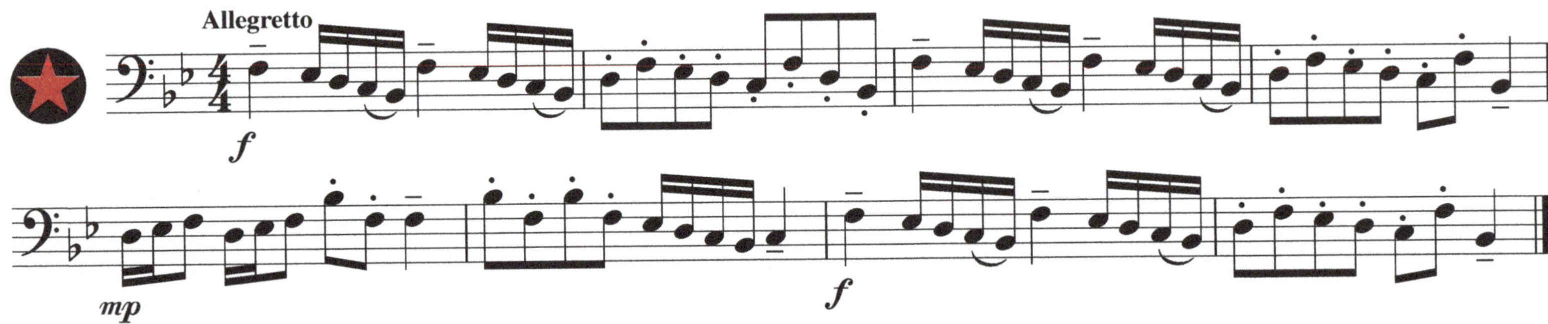

81. RHYTHM RAP
Clap
1 e & a 2 & 3 & a 4 & 1 & a 2 & 3 & a 4 & 1 & a 2 & 3 & a 4 & 1 & a 2 & 3 & 4 &
82. MARCHING ALONG
1 e & a 2 & 3 & a 4 & 1 & a 2 & 3 & a 4 & 1 & a 2 & 3 & a 4 & 1 & a 2 & 3 & 4 &
83. FANFARE FOR BAND – Trio
Maestoso
A
B
C
f
84. O TANNENBAUM
German Carol
Andante
mp
1.
2.
mf
f
rall.
85. S'VIVON Use A♭ major scale fingering.
Traditional Hanukkah Song
Moderato
mf
f
mp
f
mp
86. GOOD KING WENCESLAS
English Carol
Allegretto
mf
rit.

DAILY WARM-UPS

WORK-OUTS FOR TONE & TECHNIQUE

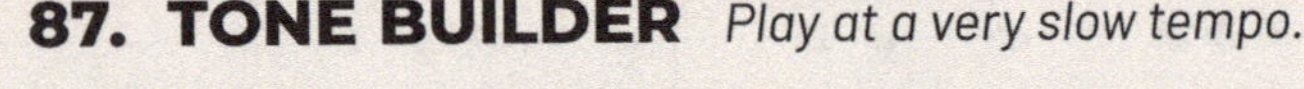

87. TONE BUILDER *Play at a very slow tempo.*

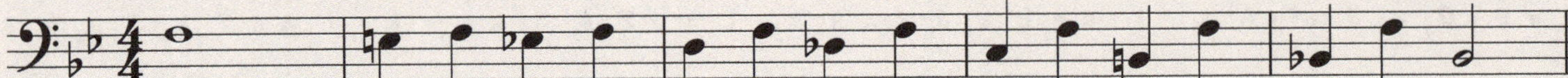

88. FLEXIBILITY STUDY

89. TECHNIQUE TRAX *Use A♭ major scale fingering.*

90. CHORALE

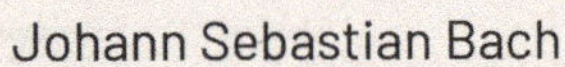

Johann Sebastian Bach

HISTORY

French composer **Georges Bizet** (1838–1875) entered the Paris Conservatory to study music when he was only ten years old. There he won many awards for voice, piano, organ, and composition. Bizet's best known composition is the opera *Carmen*, which was first performed in 1875. *Carmen* tells the story of a band of Gypsies, soldiers, smugglers, and outlaws. Originally criticized for its realism on stage, it was soon hailed as the most popular French opera ever written.

91. TOREADOR SONG (from CARMEN)

Georges Bizet

92. LA CUMPARSITA

G. Rodriguez

Moderato

mf

5th fret D string

Enharmonics

93. THE YELLOW ROSE OF TEXAS

Check the key signature. Use A♭ major scale fingering.

American Folk Song

Moderato

mf

E♭ Major Scale Fingering

5fr

THEORY

94. SCALE STUDY – New Note

Try E♭ major scale fingering.

E♭

8fr

E♭ Scale

E♭

Check rhythm

Until 1974 Australia's official national anthem was *God Save The Queen*. A competition was held in 1973 to compose a new anthem, but none of the entries met with the judges' approval. Finally the government asked the public to vote, choosing from among Australia's 3 most popular patriotic songs. After easily defeating *Waltzing Matilda* and *God Save The Queen*, *Advance Australia Fair* was officially declared the national anthem of Australia on April 19, 1974.

HISTORY

95. ADVANCE AUSTRALIA FAIR

Peter Dodds McCormick

96. ESSENTIAL CREATIVITY

Arrange the melody of "America (My Country 'Tis Of Thee)" for your instrument. Write out the first line (6 measures). Your first note is F. ADD: Key signature—key of F • Time signature—3/4 • Tempo and dynamic markings.

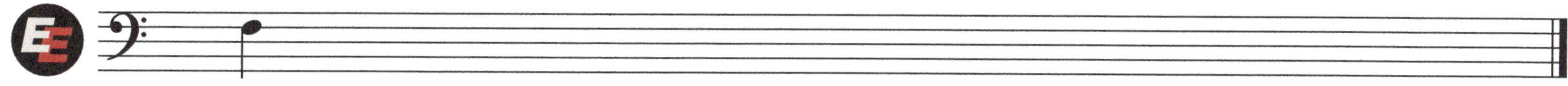

Play the completed line on your instrument to hear your own version.

97. AMERICAN PATROL

F. W. Meacham

98. ARIA (from MARRIAGE OF FIGARO)

Wolfgang Amadeus Mozart

HISTORY

American composer **John Philip Sousa** (1854–1932) was best known for his brilliant band marches. Sousa wrote 136 marches, including *The Stars and Stripes Forever*, which was declared the official march of the United States of America in 1987.

99. THE STARS AND STRIPES FOREVER

John Philip Sousa

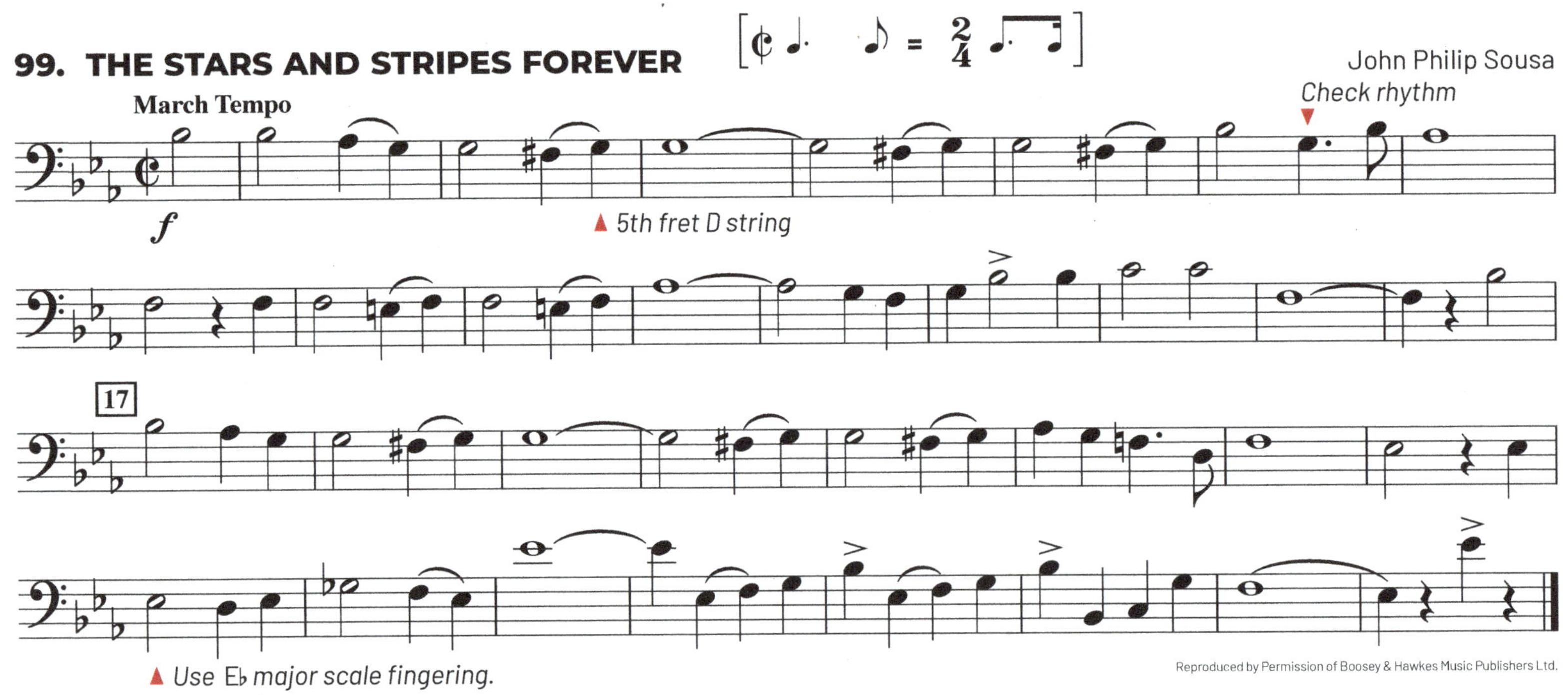

100. SIGHTREADING CHALLENGE *Remember the S-T-A-R-S guidelines.*

THEORY

$\frac{6}{8}$ Time Signature

$\frac{6}{8}$ = **6 beats** per measure
= **Eighth** note gets one beat

♪ = 1 beat ♩ = 2 beats
♩. = 3 beats 𝅗𝅥. = 6 beats

6/8 time is usually played with a slight emphasis on the **1st** and **4th** beats of each measure. This divides the measure into 2 groups of 3 beats each. In faster music, these two primary beats will make the music feel like it's counted "in 2."

101. RHYTHM RAP *Clap the rhythm while counting and tapping.*

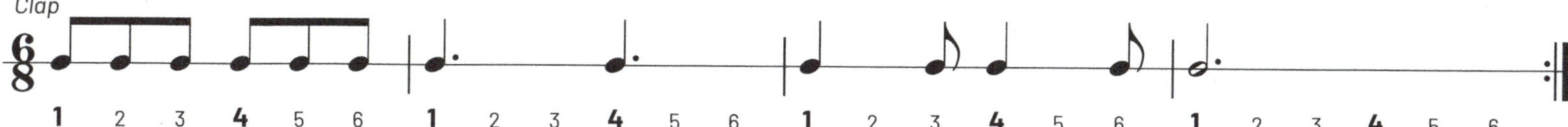

102. LAZY DAY

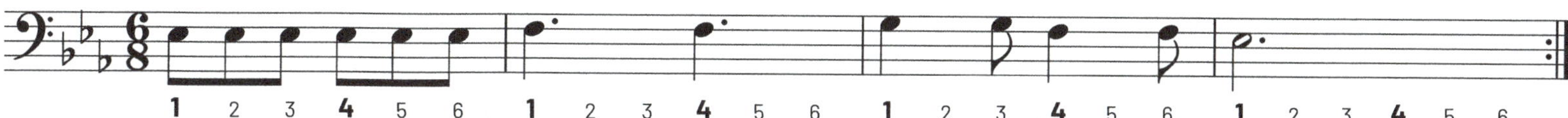

103. ROW YOUR BOAT

104. JOLLY GOOD FELLOW

105. CHANSON

French Folk Song

106. ESSENTIAL ELEMENTS QUIZ – WHEN JOHNNY COMES MARCHING HOME

American Folk Song

THEORY

More Enharmonics

Remember that notes which sound the same but have different letter names are called **enharmonics**. These are some common enharmonics that you'll use in the exercises below.

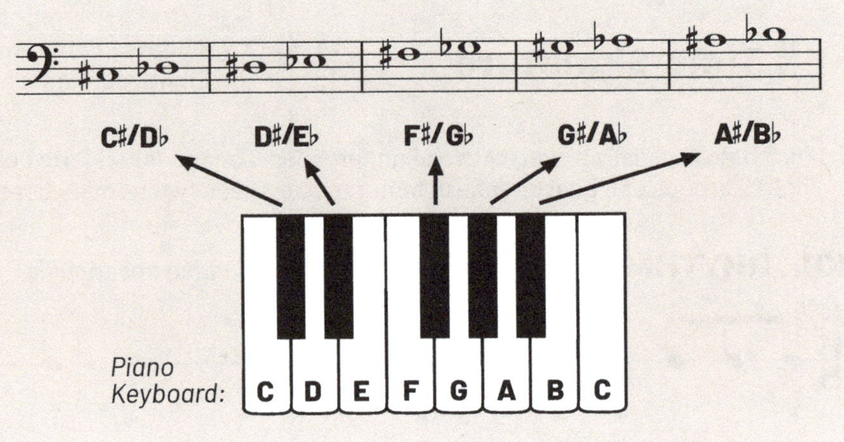

More Chromatics

The smallest distance between two notes is a half-step, and a scale made up of consecutive half-steps is a **chromatic scale**. These are usually written with **enharmonic** notes—sharps when going up and flats when going down.

107. CHROMATIC SCALE

Practice slowly until you are sure of all the fingerings.

108. TECHNIQUE TRAX

HISTORY

A **Habañera** is a Cuban dance and song form in slow 2/4 meter. It is named after the city of Havana, the capital of Cuba. Made popular in the New World in the early 19th Century, it was later carried over to Spain. There the rhythms of the Habañera were incorporated into many styles of Latin music. One of the most famous Habañeras is heard in Bizet's *Carmen*, written in 1875.

109. HABAÑERA (from CARMEN)

Georges Bizet

110. CHROMATIC CRESCENDO

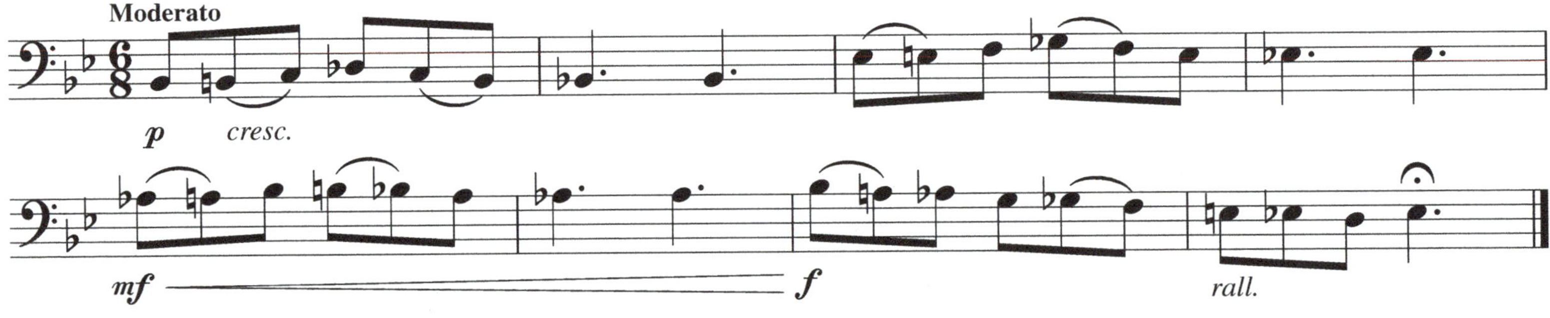

111. TURKISH MARCH (from THE RUINS OF ATHENS)

Ludwig van Beethoven

Allegretto

mf

112. THE OVERLANDER

Australian Folk Song

Allegro

mp ▲ 5th to 6th fret on A string

113. STACCATO STUDY

Moderato

▼ D♭ Enharmonic

p *cresc.*

f *decresc.* *p*

114. YANKEE DOODLE DANDY

Words and Music by George M. Cohan

Allegro

mf *mp*

f

17

mf

mp *f*

115. SIGHTREADING CHALLENGE

Remember the **S-T-A-R-S** guidelines:
S – Sharps or flats in the key signature, **T** – Time signature and tempos, **A** – Accidentals, **R** – Rhythm, **S** – Signs

Triplets

A **triplet** is a group of **3** notes played in the space of **2**. In $\frac{2}{4}$, $\frac{3}{4}$, or $\frac{4}{4}$ time, an eighth note triplet is spread evenly across one beat.

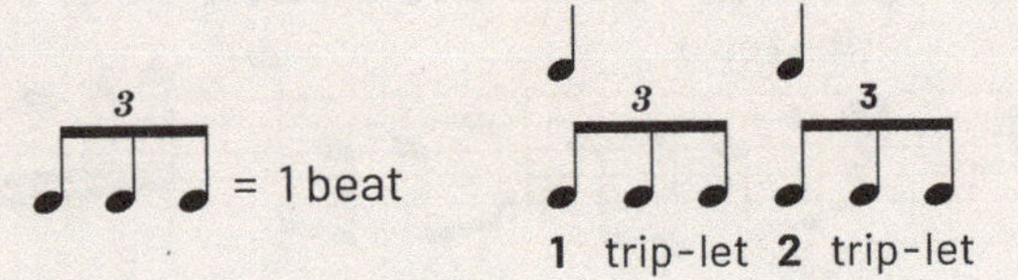

116. RHYTHM RAP

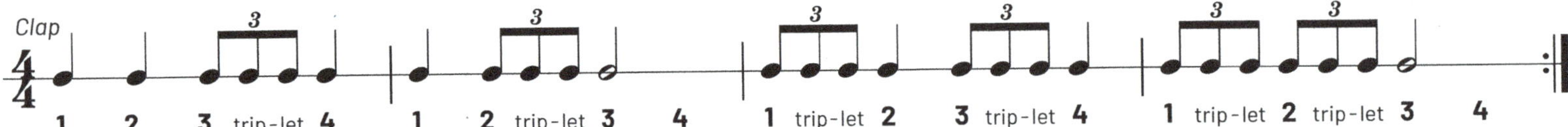

117. THREE TO GET READY

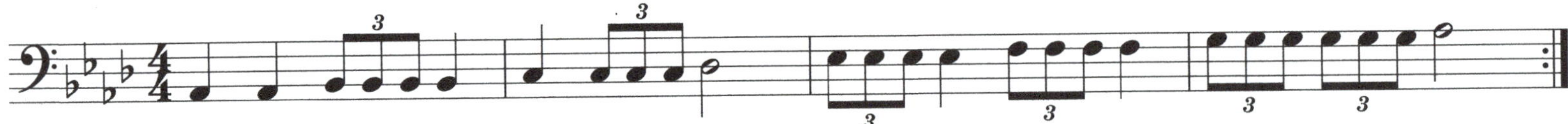

118. TRIPLET STUDY

119. MARCH (from THE NUTCRACKER) – Duet

Peter I. Tchaikovsky

120. ESSENTIAL ELEMENTS QUIZ – THEME FROM FAUST

Charles Gounod

F Major Scale Fingering

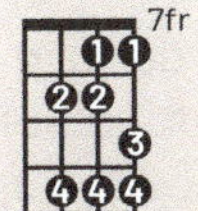

121. SCALE STUDY – New Notes *Try F major scale fingering.*

E 9fr

F 10fr

F Scale

▼ E ▼ F

▲ *Check Rhythm*

122. OVER THE RIVER AND THROUGH THE WOODS *Try F major scale fingering.*

American Folk Song

Allegretto

mf *f* *decresc.*

1. 2.

123. RHYTHM RAP

124. ON THE MOVE

125. HIGHER GROUND

126. ESSENTIAL ELEMENTS QUIZ

HISTORY

The first known printing of the lyrics and music to **The Marines' Hymn** dates from August 1, 1918. An unknown author is believed to have taken the opening words of the song from the words on the Marine Corps flag, "From the halls of Montezuma to the shores of Tripoli." The music was taken from "Genevieve de Brabant," by the operetta composer Jacques Offenbach.

127. THE MARINES' HYMN

D.S. al Fine

Play until you see the **D.S. al Fine**. Then go back to the sign (𝄋) and play until the word **Fine**. **D.S.** is the abbreviation for **Dal Segno**, or "from the sign," and **Fine** means "the end."

128. D.S. MARCH *Use E♭ major scale fingering.*

Accelerando

accel. – Gradually faster.

129. CAN-CAN

Jacques Offenbach

▲ *Watch your director.*

130. TARANTELLA

Italian Folk Song

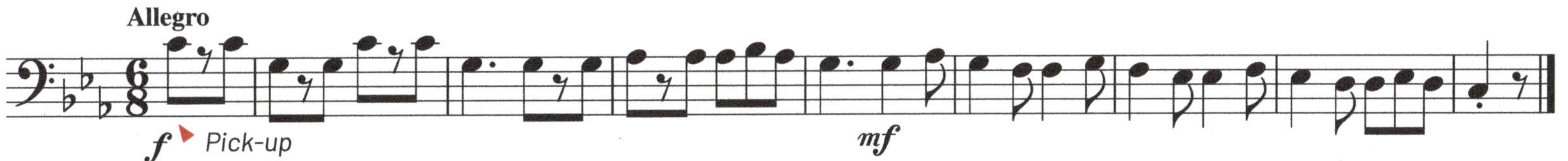

The **waltz** is a dance in moderate 3/4 time which developed around 1800 from the Ländler, an Austrian peasant dance. Austrian composer **Johann Strauss, Jr.** (1825–1899) composed over 400 waltzes. These include such famous pieces as *The Blue Danube*, *Tales From the Vienna Woods* and *Emperor Waltz*.

131. EMPEROR WALTZ

Johann Strauss, Jr.

Legato Style

legato – Played in a smooth, connected style.

132. ENGLISH DANCE – Duet

Johann Christian Bach

133. ESSENTIAL ELEMENTS QUIZ – BRITISH GRENADIERS

Traditional

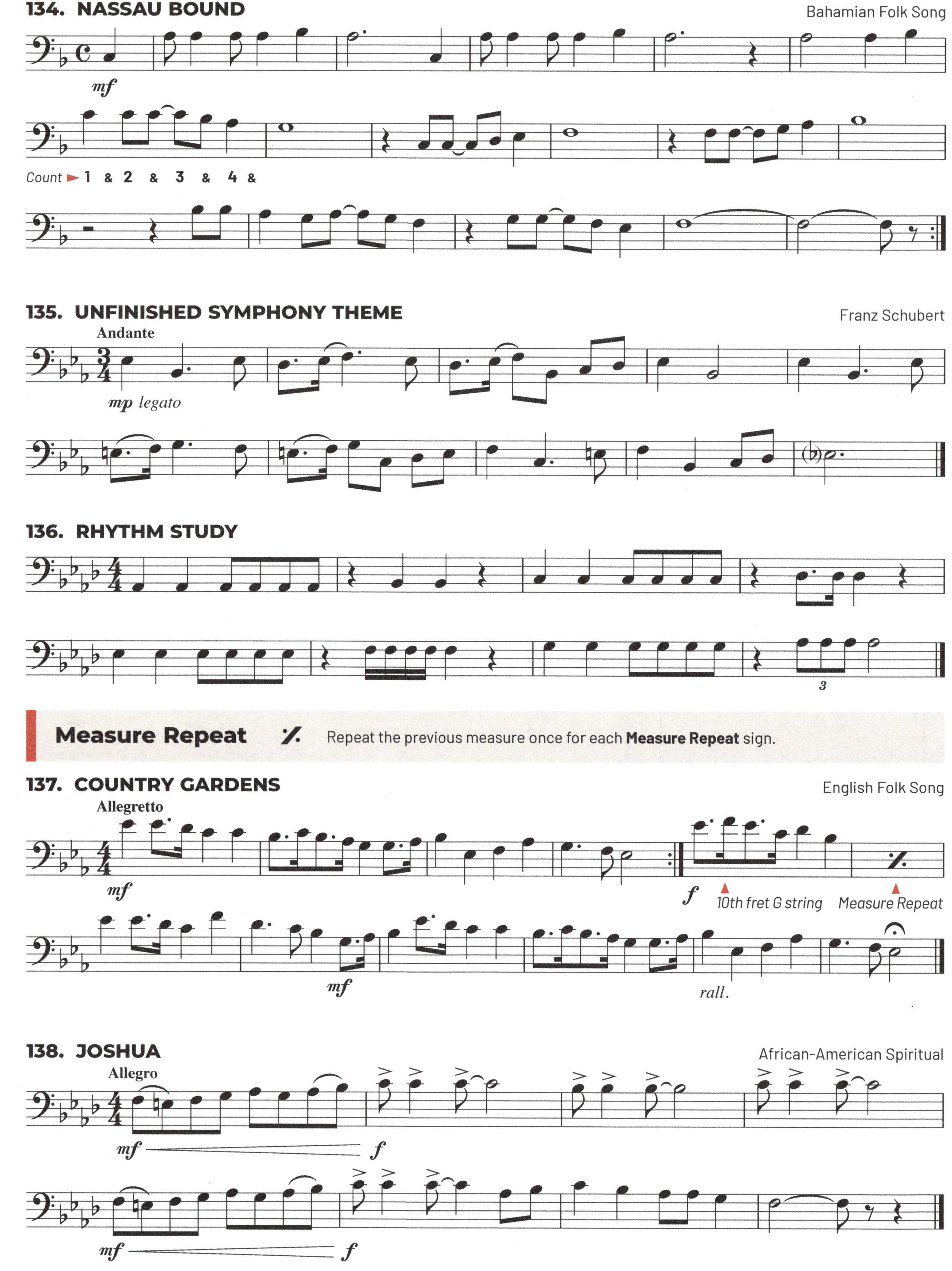
134. NASSAU BOUND
Bahamian Folk Song
mf
Count ► 1 & 2 & 3 & 4 &
135. UNFINISHED SYMPHONY THEME
Franz Schubert
Andante
mp legato
136. RHYTHM STUDY
3
Measure Repeat
Repeat the previous measure once for each Measure Repeat sign.
137. COUNTRY GARDENS
English Folk Song
Allegretto
mf
f
10th fret G string
Measure Repeat
mf
rall.
138. JOSHUA
African-American Spiritual
Allegro
mf
f
mf
f

139. LISTEN TO THE MOCKINGBIRD
Alice Hawthorne
Moderato
mf
Pick-up
140. ANCHORS AWEIGH
Capt. A.H. Miles and C.A. Zimmerman
March Tempo
f
mf
cresc.
1.
2.
f
f
141. GREENSLEEVES
Use A♭ major scale fingering.
English Folk Song
Andante
p
mf
8th fret G string
rit.
142. THE LONG CLIMB
Measure Repeat
143. THE BLUE BELLS OF SCOTLAND
Scottish Folk Song
Moderato
f
1.
2.
mf
f

THEORY

Major and Minor

The scales you've already learned are called **Major** scales. They all follow the same pattern, with **half-steps** between notes 3-4 and between notes 7-8.

Natural Minor scales follow a different pattern, with **half-steps** between notes 2-3 and 5-6. The **G Minor** scale uses the same key signature as **B♭ Major**.

Another type of minor scale is called **Harmonic Minor**, which adds an accidental to raise the **7th** note by a half-step. Compare the scales on the right.

See page 37 for additional minor scales.

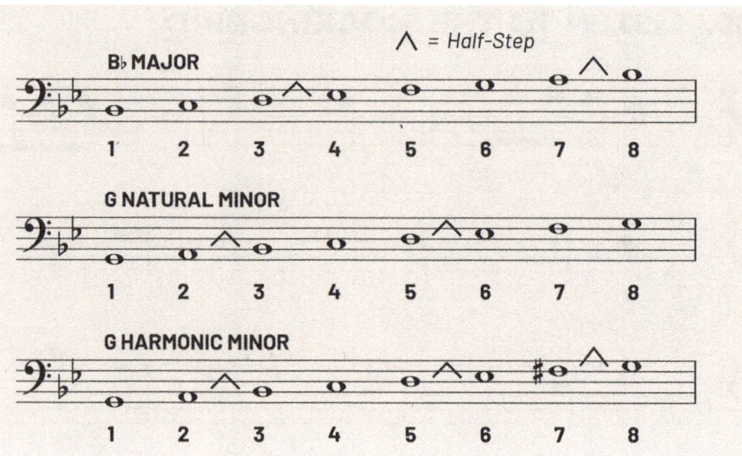

144. NATURAL MINOR SCALE

145. FINALE FROM "NEW WORLD SYMPHONY"

Antonin Dvorák

146. HARMONIC MINOR SCALE

147. HUNGARIAN DANCE NO. 5

Johannes Brahms

148. POMP AND CIRCUMSTANCE (LAND OF HOPE AND GLORY)

Edward Elgar

PERFORMANCE SPOTLIGHT

D.S. al Coda

Play until you see the **D.S. al Coda**. Then go back to the sign (𝄋) and play until the **Coda Sign** ("To Coda" 𝄌). Skip directly to the **Coda** and play until the end.

PERFORMANCE SPOTLIGHT

151. DANNY BOY – Band Arrangement

Irish Folk Song
Arr. by John Higgins

Additional Bonus Songs are available online. See the inside front cover for details.

PERFORMANCE SPOTLIGHT

153. SERENGETI (AFRICAN RHAPSODY) – Band Arrangement

John Higgins

RUBANK® STUDIES

RUBANK® STUDIES

KEY OF E♭

163. *Use E♭ major scale fingering.*

164. *Use E♭ major scale fingering.*

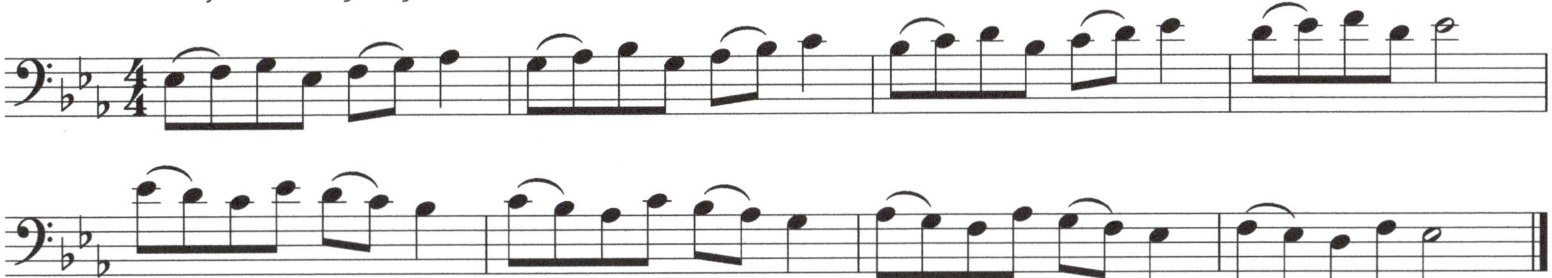

165.

166. *Use E♭ major scale fingering.*

KEY OF F

167. *Use F major scale fingering.*

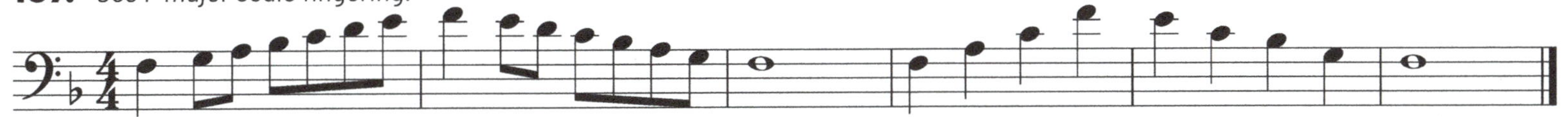

168.

169.

170. *Use F major scale fingering.*

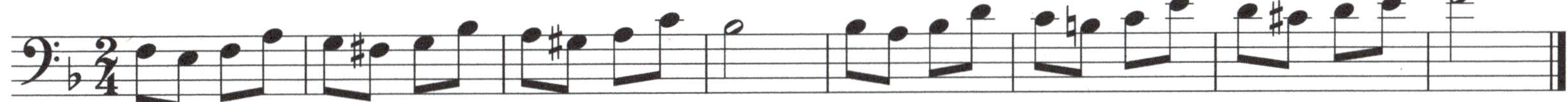

RUBANK® STUDIES

KEY OF A♭

171. *Use A♭ major scale fingering.*

172. *Use A♭ major scale fingering.*

173. *Use A♭ major scale fingering.*

174. *Use A♭ major scale fingering.*

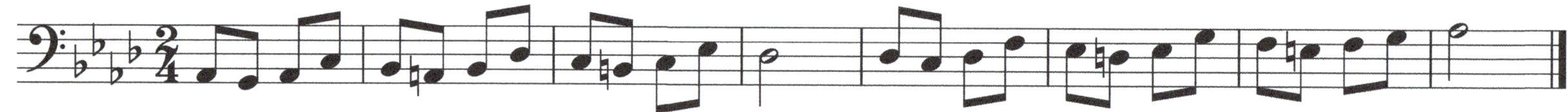

KEY OF C

175.

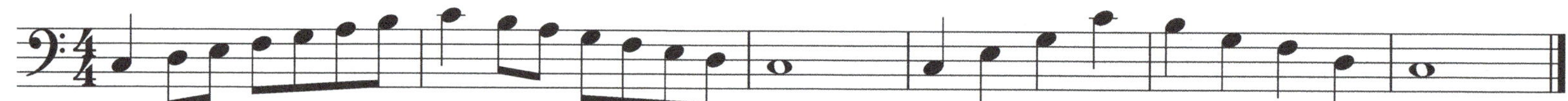

176. *Try without using open strings.*

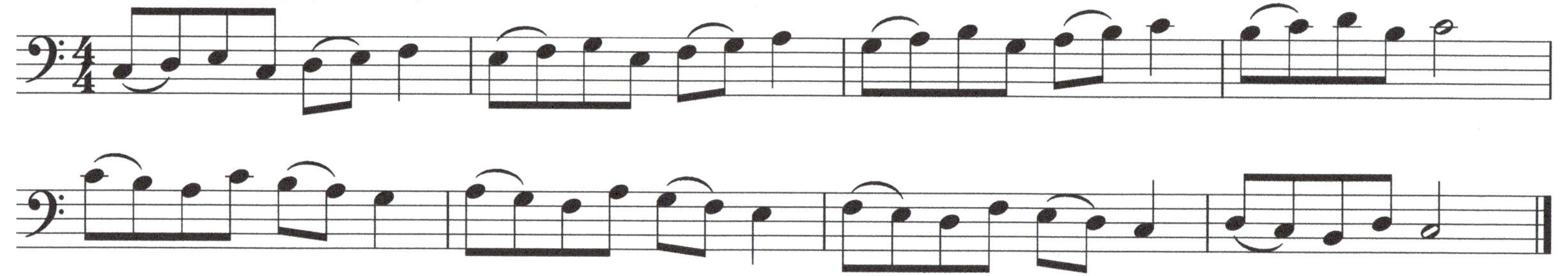

177.

178.

RUBANK® STUDIES

KEY OF G MINOR

179.

180.

KEY OF C MINOR

181.

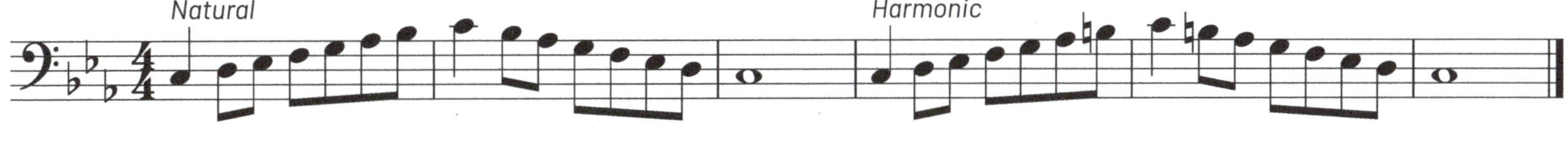

182.

KEY OF D MINOR

183.

184.

CHROMATIC SCALES

185.

186.

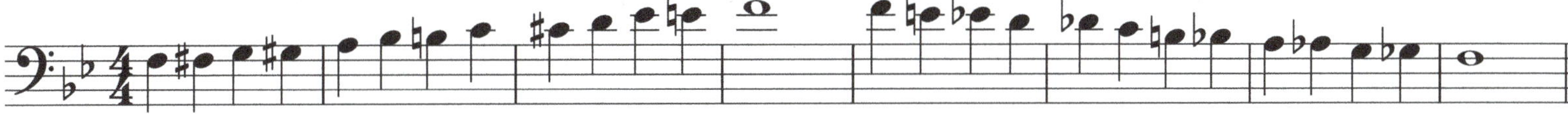

INDIVIDUAL STUDY – Electric Bass

187. LOW NOTE EXCURSION – New Note

188. LOW ENHARMONIC STUDY – New Note

189. MELODY PATTERNS

190. ARPEGGIO CHALLENGE

191. STUDY IN A♭ *Use A♭ major scale fingering.*

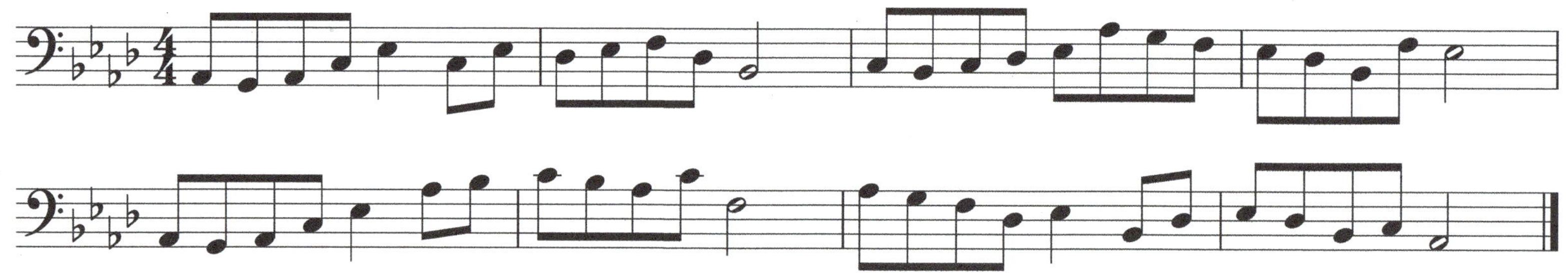

192. CHROMATIC ETUDE

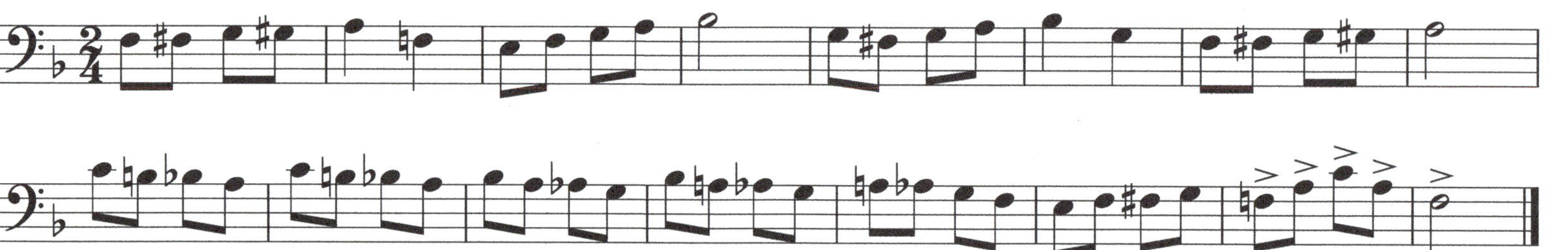

INDIVIDUAL STUDY – Electric Bass

193. TECHNIQUE BUILDER #1

194. TECHNIQUE BUILDER #2

195. TECHNIQUE BUILDER #3

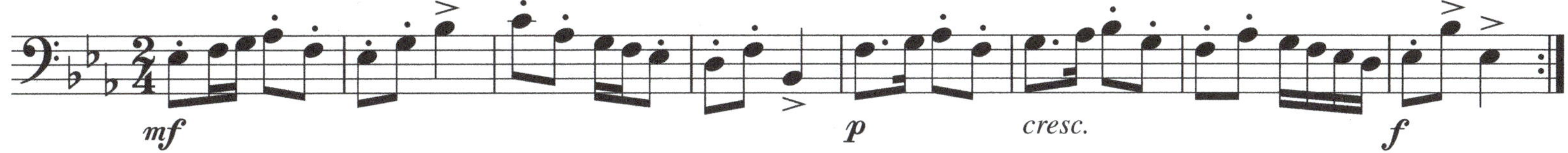

196. TRIPLET ETUDE

197. BASIC BLUES PATTERNS

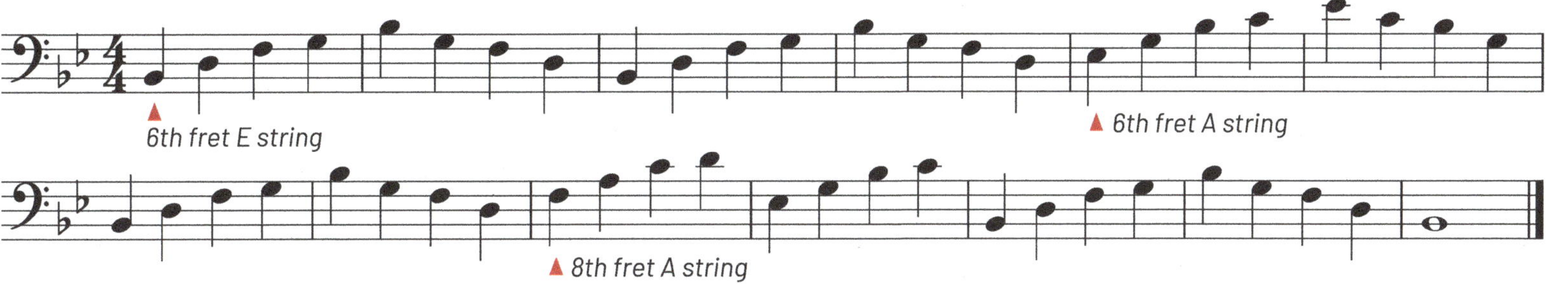

198. BLUES PATTERNS WITH 6ths & 7ths

199. CHROMATIC BLUES PATTERNS

INDIVIDUAL STUDY – Electric Bass

Solo with Piano Accompaniment

You can perform this solo with the piano accompaniment on the following page.

200. IN THE HALL OF THE MOUNTAIN KING from "Peer Gynt Suite" – Electric Bass Solo

Online audio – see inside front cover to access.

Edvard Grieg
Arr. by G.E. Holmes

INDIVIDUAL STUDY – Electric Bass

200. IN THE HALL OF THE MOUNTAIN KING from "Peer Gynt Suite" – Piano accompaniment

Online audio – see inside front cover to access.

Edvard Grieg
Arr. by G.E. Holmes

RHYTHM STUDIES

RHYTHM STUDIES

CREATING MUSIC

Theme and Variation

Theme and Variation is a technique used by composers and arrangers to create interesting musical ideas that are "varied" from an established melody, or "theme." Play the following theme and two variations to hear how the arranger has created new phrases based on the original melody.

1. THEME

"Simple Gifts"

VARIATION 1 *Adding some notes • Changing some rhythms*

VARIATION 2 *Removing notes • Changing rhythms • Adding accents • Adding notes*

2. THEME AND YOUR VARIATION

Write your own variation of this theme. Use your instrument to hear and try different ideas.

"Candy Mountain Rock"

Theme

Your Variation

Blues Improvisation

Improvisation using a **Blues Scale** is an important part of jazz and popular music. Musicians use combinations of these notes and various rhythms to create their own spontaneous solos over a 12 measure progression of chords.

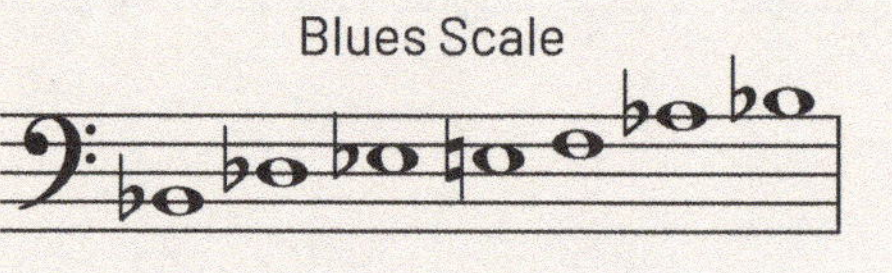

3. LET'S JAM

Use the indicated notes from the Blues Scale to create your own solo to play with the accompaniment (Line B).

You can mark your progress through the book on this page.
Fill in the stars as instructed by your band director.

1. Page 2–4, Review
2. Page 5, Sightreading Challenge, No. 19
3. Page 6, Daily Warm-Ups
4. Page 7, Sightreading Challenge, No. 31
5. Page 8, Essential Creativity, No. 38
6. Page 9, EE Quiz, No. 43
7. Page 10, Sightreading Challenge, No. 49
8. Page 11, EE Quiz, No. 55
9. Page 12–13, Performance Spotlight
10. Page 15, EE Quiz, No. 74
11. Page 16, Sightreading Challenge, No. 80
12. Page 18, Daily Warm-Ups
13. Page 19, Essential Creativity, No. 96
14. Page 20, Sightreading Challenge, No. 100
15. Page 21, EE Quiz, No. 106
16. Page 22, Chromatic Scale, No. 107
17. Page 23, Sightreading Challenge, No. 115
18. Page 24, EE Quiz, No. 120
19. Page 25, EE Quiz, No. 126
20. Page 27, EE Quiz, No. 133
21. Page 30, Natural Minor Scale, No. 144
22. Page 30, Harmonic Minor Scale, No. 146
23. Page 30, Pomp and Circumstance, No. 148
24. Page 31, Performance Spotlight
25. Page 32, Performance Spotlight
26. Page 33, Performance Spotlight
27. Page 38–39, Individual Study
28. Page 40, Performance Spotlight

MUSIC — AN ESSENTIAL ELEMENT OF LIFE

FINGERING CHART

ELECTRIC BASS

Instrument Care Reminders

- Be sure your amplifier is turned off before plugging-in or unplugging the audio cable connecting it to your instrument.
- When unplugging a cable, hold it by the plug (not by the wire).
- After playing, wipe off the instrument and strings with a clean soft cloth. Return the instrument to its case.
- Close all the latches on your case when the instrument is inside.
- Keep all 4 strings in tune (at normal tension) to prevent warping of the neck.
- Your case is designed to hold only specific objects. If you force anything else into the case, it may damage your instrument.

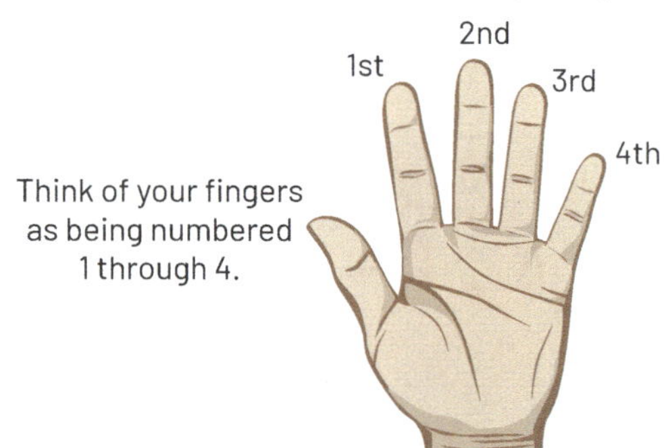

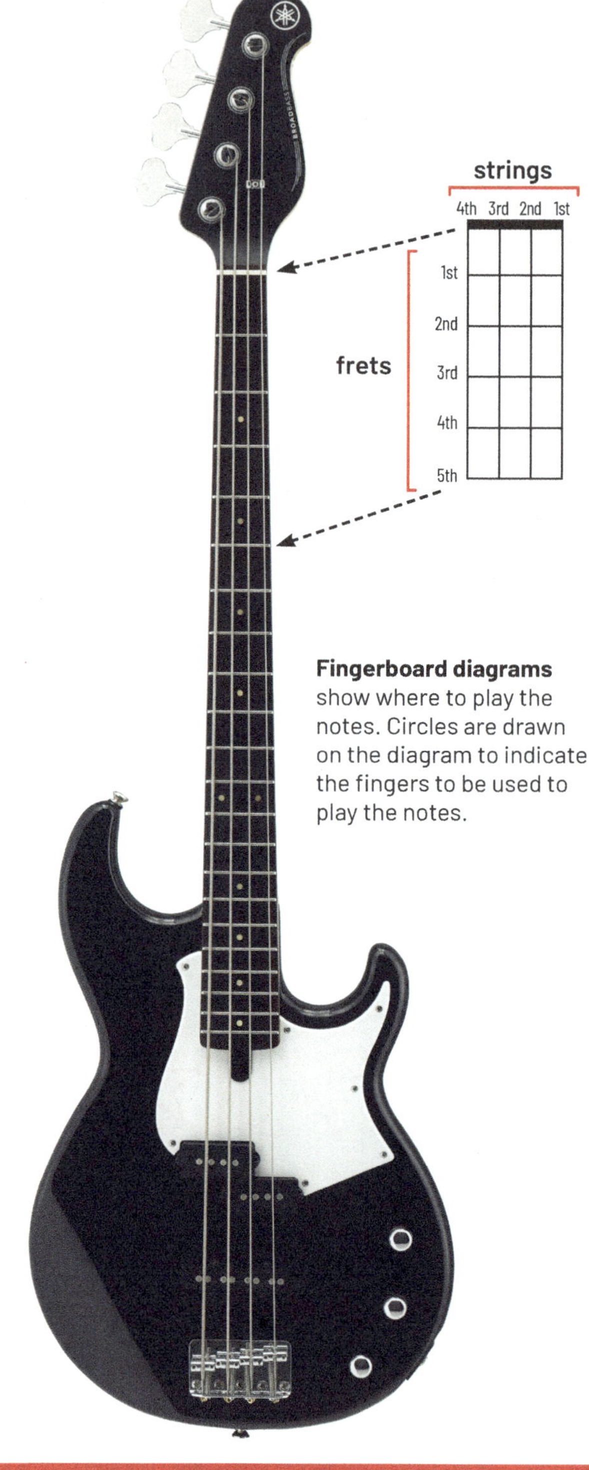

Fingerboard diagrams show where to play the notes. Circles are drawn on the diagram to indicate the fingers to be used to play the notes.

Instruments and photos courtesy of Yamaha.

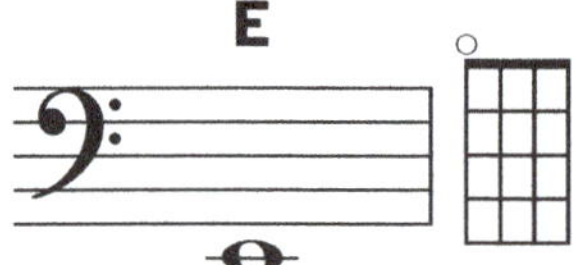

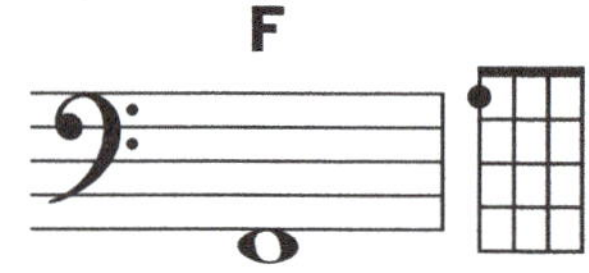

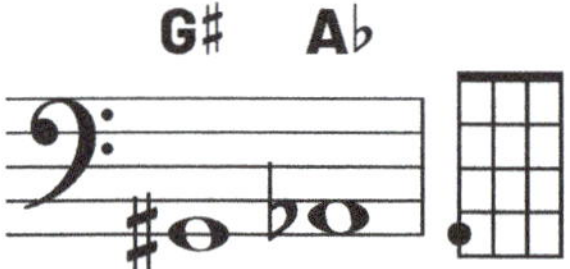

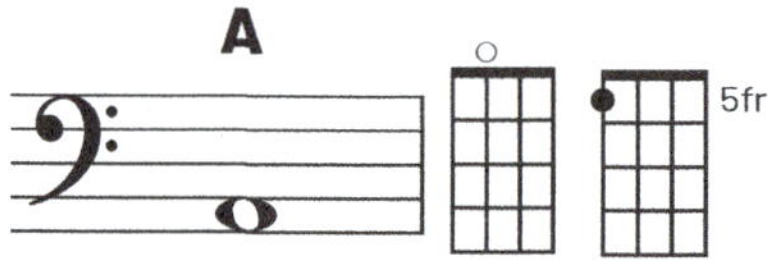

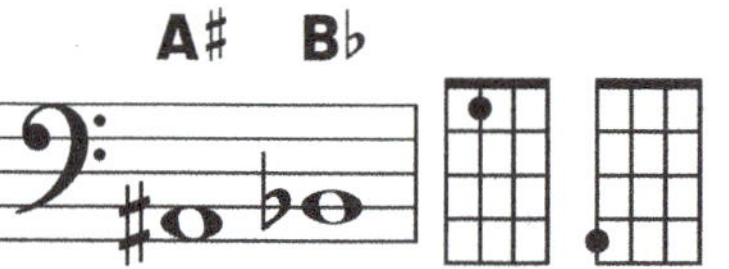

FINGERING CHART

ELECTRIC BASS

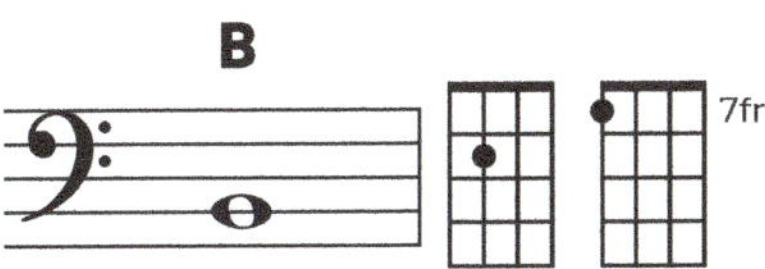

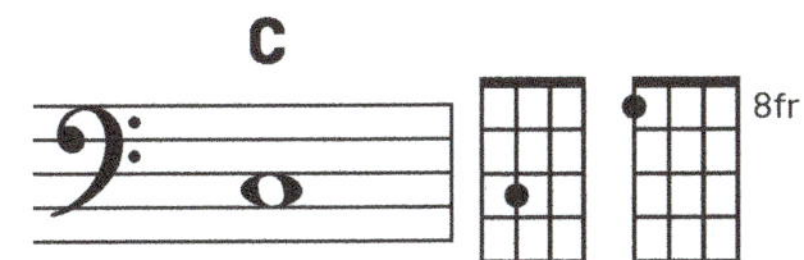

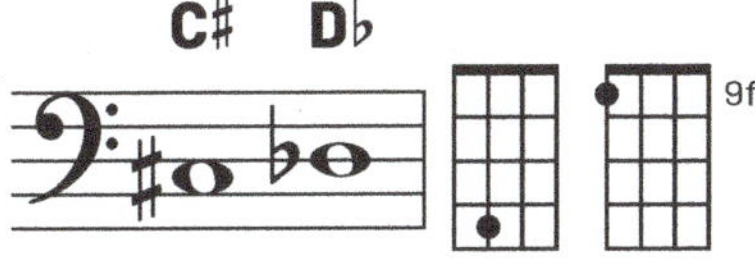

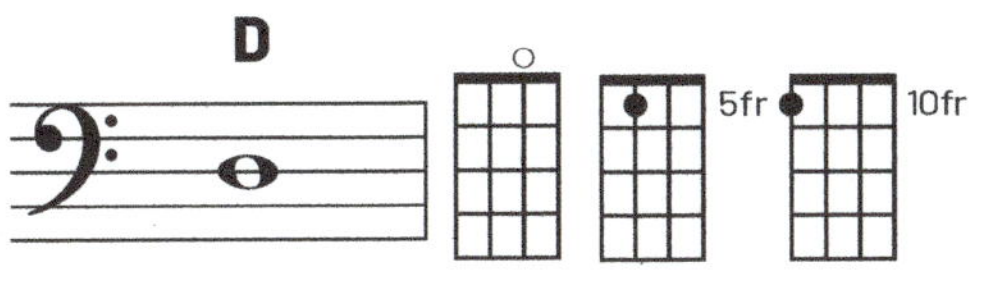

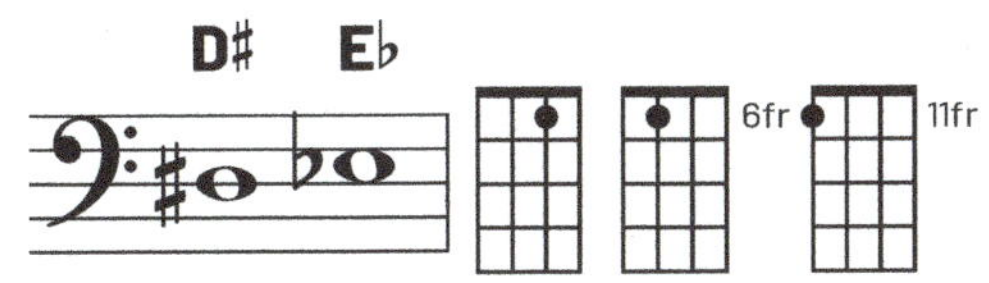

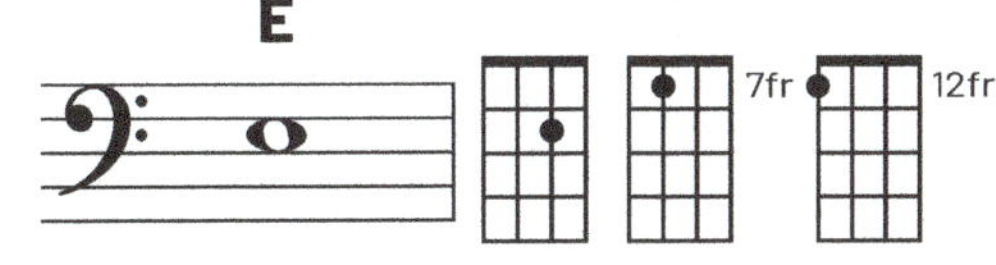

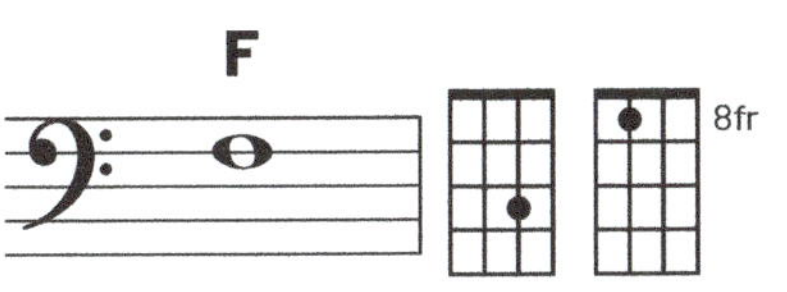

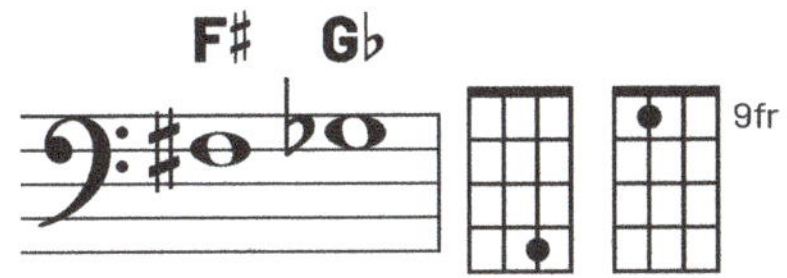

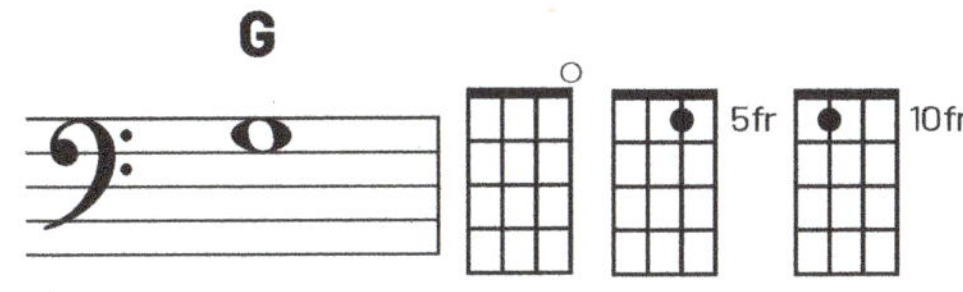

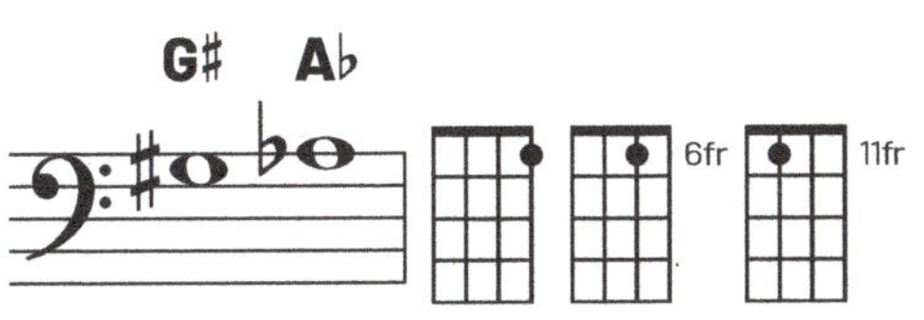

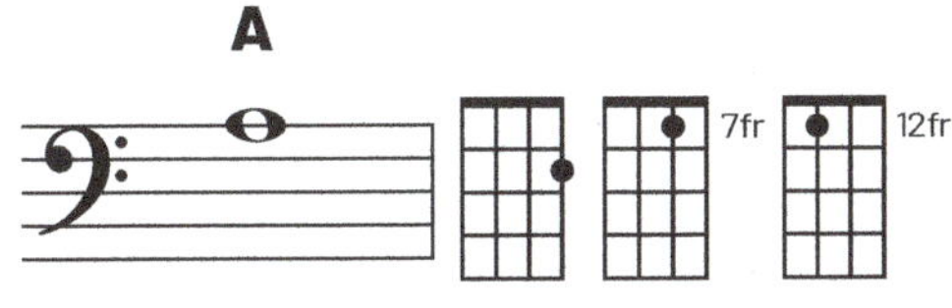

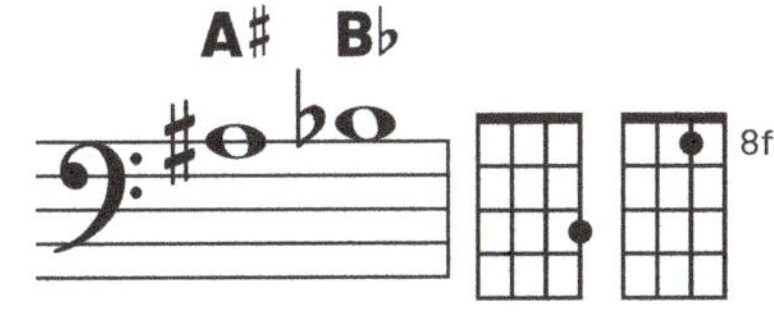

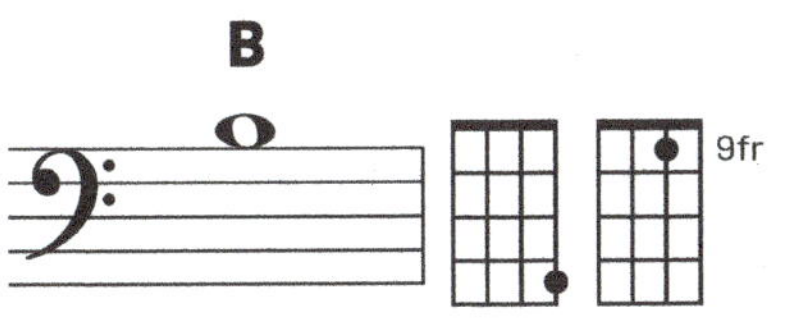

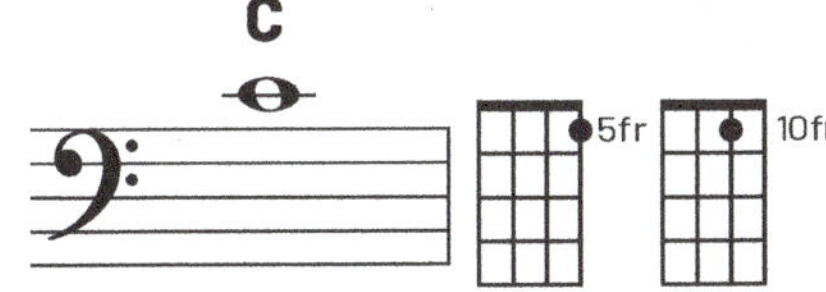

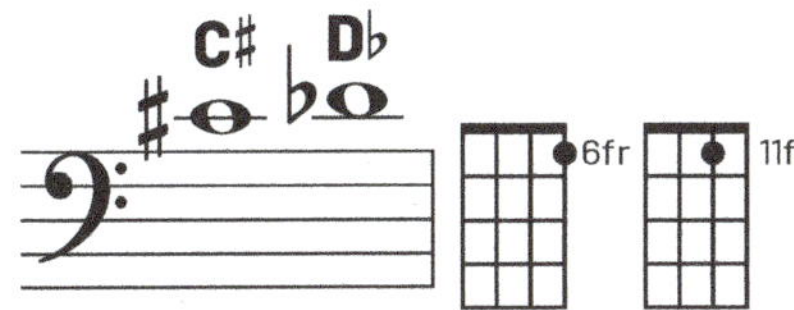

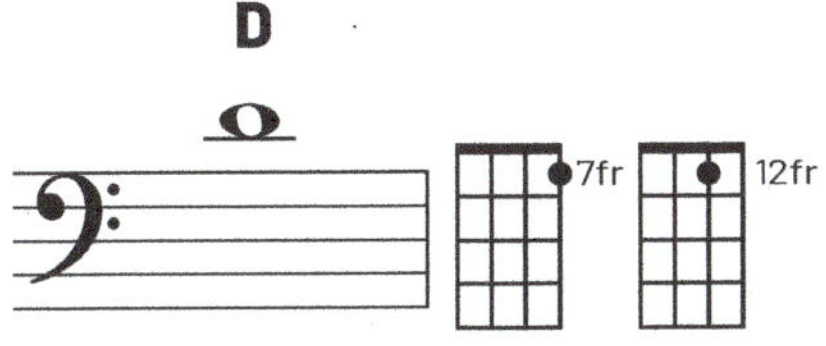

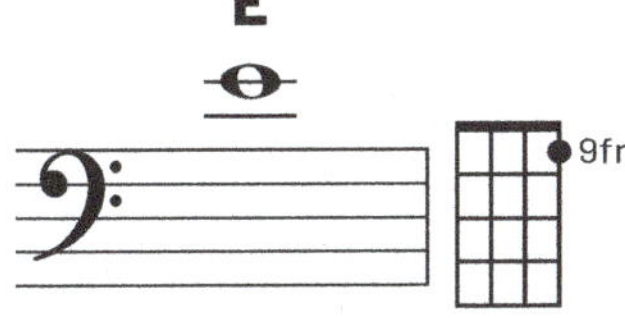

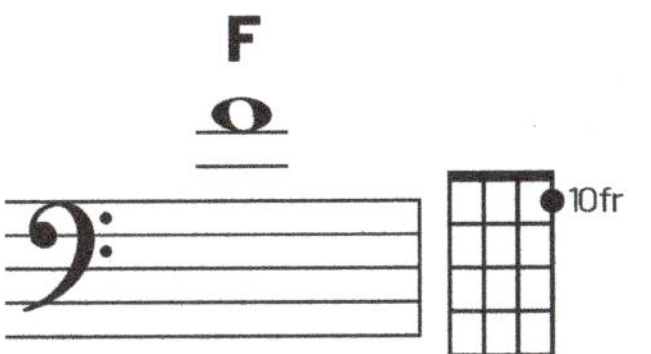

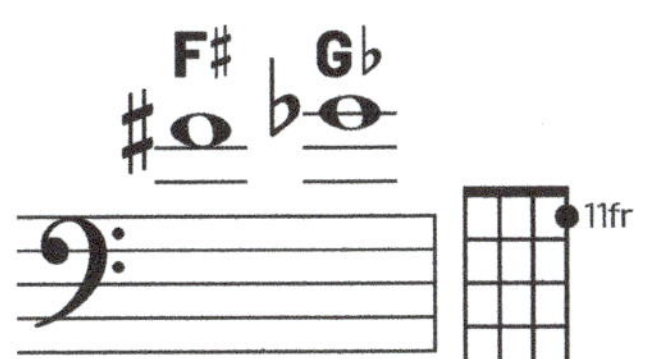

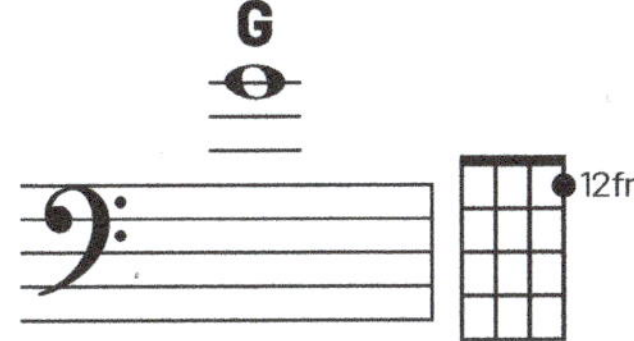

Reference Index

Definitions (pg.)

Book 1 Review

Composers

World Music